Anna O'Reilly

A Box of Broken Crayons

Anna O'Reilly

For your caged inner child,
Whose imagination has been told no

Anna O'Reilly

Contents

Anna O'Reilly

Fresh

Wax

Anna O'Reilly

A Box Of Broken Crayons

Your legs are stumps of clay
Not yet molded
They will take you far one day
But be careful of the water
That might get in your way

You have been painted with life
Colors the naked eye can't see
But be careful of the water
That might get in your way

You have been folded into an airplane
Eager for your goals to fly further than any bird
But be careful of the water
That might get in your way

You have been spilled over the table of creation
Hydrating the blend of colors until
They become brown
Coated by clay
As you are asked to make it all go away
Still a masterpiece in the child's eye
But be careful of the adults' view
That might get in your way

A lullaby is sung to the apple farms
As gray turns to rainbow
Changing the color in your eyes
They are not only rich in amber syrup
Have not fallen like brown leaves
Are not buried emeralds
They are much more than each color presented
If you examine past the base lens
You may see reflections of four-leaf clovers
Kindness in a tsunami of terror
Comfort of an oversized knitted sweater
Resemblance of a sunset after a serene rain
Health of dirt that grows each continent
Perfection stronger than color dares replicate
As you hold more than your eye color
Though I'm curious
Can you see a soft manuka honey breeze
Nip at your arm
To welcome you
Or observe fears that do not exist yet
Are you greeted by the sight of strangers
Can you see their intentions heavy in their souls
Or do they need to sing lullabies
As your ears may be more equipped to read those

I am aware you may not have seen the color of life yet
But I want to show you the rainbow
Let me explain the red roses
You will hope to be given
The same ones full of empty promises
Yet always the first to be picked
You will observe the pumpkins' orange tint
Carved into faces
A representation of the pieces you will never get back
Yet you will try
You will never see yellow as it's neglected
But spoken for
Yet you will always see it as the happiest color
You will be covered in internal bruises
Imitating the purple and blue
These are the injuries you will one day find safety in
Yet the ones you will always say sorry for

You must not stray far from the rainbow
As these are the colors we use
To paint the stories of who we are
What was supposed to be a masterpiece
Is now an abstract mess
That even I am still learning to love

When you awoke fragile and calm
I was unaware of the life you could bring
Not only inside your small vessel
But to the days rooted in solitude

From birth
You have climbed the jungle gym
On the scorching playground
Before you could even talk
You attempted to grip the bars
Unable to touch more than air
As you diligently stepped on each piece of metal
Hung from your calluses
Weird to think that what once seemed hard
Brings us the wish of childhood
Along with tears of harder struggles

The jungle gym I once climbed
Taught me a lesson that I never wanted to learn
Let each breath not be wasted
On the anticipating view that takes it away
But rather let yourself breathe
On the tedious journey
Along the way

A thousand miles away
Lost in the mysterious sea
You will still be a part of me
I do not need to chase every land you explore
For I was the first to count your toes
That walked along the old shore
I was the first to show you the stories
That you hold in your pack
Providing you lessons
That it would be a shame if you gave back
I was the first to give your eyes the light
When you were without the sun
So you can still see my love for you along the stars
The same ones we once paced under together

But if we are being honest
I was also the first to say goodbye
As adventure is what you craved
Since you first broke free of my arms
I taught you all that I could
I let you go
With trust that each hug I provided
Was enough love to provide security
And the epitome of approval

Outside the Lines

Last night I explored the archives of my past
I found a shard of glass
Stained with a rich liquid more vicious than water
That may have unsealed my eyes to spring a leak
Causing my reaction to pain
Painting the world with colors
I doubt we see the same

I found the first flower I ever picked
A dandelion
Plucked from its home upon a root
A change in texture
In the very spot a bee once drank from
A flower that bloomed with me
The same night it died
Discovering it would leave me too

I found the little child I once knew
While I explored the archives of my past
Regretting it soon after
As I felt I was betraying my child once again

To my inner child
I must apologize
We have not talked since the pain of exclusion
Became of unease

Anticipating that like tears
I would wipe you away
Only for you to continue to flow
Then you didn't return
That's when I knew
I had let my childhood
Slip too fast
Missing my chance
For a proper goodbye

Oh my lost child
Have you been misdirected
Taken down the wrong road

I have searched the streets of myself to find you
Listening for your distinct laugh
Only to hear the whistle of the wind

I will keep searching
No matter the path I am led down

I have a suspicion that
You have found a home in the museum

I struggle to check
Refusing to face the idea that
You have become history

Dear little me
I know you must be mad
As you disappeared under my care
But I have questions
That I must know

So tell me dear
Where have you gone
Are you fed with your own well-being
Laced with dread
Has the music inside you shifted somber
Are you drowning from the gushing tears
The ones you once drank

Draw me a picture
Though I'm afraid it will be blank

Oh inner child
Can I ask
Why are the crayons shattered
Inside the small cardboard box

I don't mean to make assumptions
But did you go through the images of your life
Well I neglected you
Searching for the reason
Why you deserved such treatment

You won't find the reason
In any box of crayons

The monsters under your bed
Won't tell you

No picture book
Explains the story

Because you didn't deserve it
Time just made me think you did

Oh small child
Before you are put to bed
I must know
What gold are you digging for
In the sandbox under the scorching slide
What is your incentive to climb the playground
Already leaving your family's care
Running to explore more blades than grass
Yearning to allow your blood to experience color

Oh small child
Were you digging for humility under your burns
Were you climbing age too fast
To learn what happens next
In a book you forgot to write
Did you leave to explore a world without comfort

Oh small child
I can tell you want to walk the world on your own
So I must tell you now
Shards of glass do not open yellow
They stain red
Now off you must go
Bedtime is right around the corner

My darling
I see the tears that crawl
From the fountain of your face
Ones I promise to wipe away
To the best of my ability

Your trial is not your fault
It's an experiment
That sometimes causes you to disgrace
For the world is not constant beauty
But can be a symbol of abandonment
That climbs upon a life
Reaching out of the pain
Desperate to escape the loneliness of age
When you are not ready to fight

Oh my child
You gave trust
To a heartless world

You heard the words others said
The looks they gave to their friends
When you came around

Isolating you
Into a prison of insecurity

Captivity that dissolved your ability to trust
Bringing forth the hanging feeling
Of others' hatred towards you
Despite their friendship
As you contained yourself in silence
Internally projecting
The feelings of others
Onto yourself
As you have become your own enemy

Younger me
I hear the cries
That others shame you for
As your tears are full of pigment
Able to stain your blue dress

I hear your screams
For your throat is of fire
As you carry the knowledge
That your past was a forest
Suffocated by the flame of your own voice

I can also hear your bravery
For your fists of glass
May shatter
Though you grab the shards
Turning your defeat into a weapon
Unafraid to back down

I hear your combat
Against your fear of survival
As you are constantly tortured
With the idea of forgetting to live

Oh small child
I see you sneaking past the barriers
Avoiding each creaky plank
Eager to explore with no restraints
Turning the taste of freedom into a craving
That might burn your tongue
Like hot apple cider
Taken straight from the old mill

But dear
I encourage you
To not chug it all away
Or you will be left
With an empty cup
Along with a burn on your tongue
Only getting a taste of the excitement
That will soon go away

Like Icarus
You know not the extent of your boundaries
Gone hysterical at the idea
Too eager to explore the evergreen planes
Rebelling
As an act of independence

Know that like Icarus
Your wings are almost promised to burn
But that does not phase you
As you do not see the wax you are made of
Only your ability to leave the ground

This poem is for my inner child
I fear she did not listen
She ran
Reaching to join the wings of Icarus

She was always told to reach for the sun
In some ways I'm glad I never got to tell her
Freedom burns
Although I gave her a false sense of trust
In her wings of wax

My sweet child
I never should have let you imagine
How you would grow up
Now you hold me to a standard
Of someone who never existed

Every candle melts my soul
As the flames hold light
Making me aware of my surroundings

Like a house of fireflies
For I was the child who chased them
Though they never moved
Making them even more impossible to catch

I correct my first sentence
Every candle does not melt my soul
It melts my child
By showing her the impossible

Honey
I hear your cry to go home
But as humans
It's important to know the difference
Between a home
And a house

Our house may give us a roof
Our home welds together hearts of gold
A place where the worst storms
Bring the winds of memories
Our home is where the sunrise
Can be seen from the tent line

Our home brings the saddest goodbyes
But also brands the hellos into our hearts
Our house is one of brick
But our home is one words
Cannot build

So I'm just curious
When you cried to go home
Which did you mean

My sweet child
Do not fear age
As it's beauty you have not experienced yet

It does not have fangs or horns
So why do you turn it into a monster
It never had any interest in hiding under your bed

To my child
Whom I've left behind
Know that life is not honey
Though it can still be divine

However
You must stop grasping onto
The bee's stinger
Or honey will never have a chance to be made

Anna O'Reilly

I am scared to take another sip
As you have already burned my tongue
With the absence of childhood
A pain sugar can't cure

You caused me to chug it all away
Even though it was a drink meant to be savored

A Box Of Broken Crayons

In fifth grade
I ended the school announcements
With the quote
A smile happens in a flash
But its memory can last a lifetime

Maybe the classrooms were too loud
For anyone to hear
Or maybe I was too quiet
Nonetheless those words
Were not heard
Or at least
Not to the extent they should have been

Smiles became scarce
As we continued to grow
Memories we made throughout the years
Were not remembered by smiles we shared
But the excitement of growing up

I don't think we understood
That we celebrated something
That washed away our childhood
Leaving us in fear for the future

Before I leave
Know that as a child
I feared jumping off the playground
What if the floor was lava
We were just too naive to see it
Know that as a child
I always stretched to reach the highest apple
When apple-picking
The ones near the ground were never juicy enough
Know that as a child
I made concoctions in my grandma's kitchen
Refusing to be limited by a recipe
Know that as a child
I enjoyed chess
Only when my queen could fly
Know that as a child
I never finished any of my coloring Pages
For they felt repetitive and never-ending

Know that as a child
I never thought this current age would ever come
For time felt endless
And my imagination was too busy
To be full of the future

Inner Child: It's your turn

Me: For what

Inner Child: To take over the spotlight

Me: No you go ahead

Inner Child: Why

Me: The last light I stepped into burned out

Inner Child: It's a new light

Me: That doesn't mean it won't follow the same
pattern

Inner Child: I'm not scared of the dark

Me: You might not be scared of an hour of
blackness but I don't want to risk showing you
the feeling of eternal darkness too

My child
Are you there
I knock and scream your name
But you do not appear
I stand outside of your pictures
Waiting for an answer
Maybe you forgot how to hear

You must not recognize me
As I might as well be a stranger
For we have not met
These versions of each other

I have started to lose your song in my memory
Knowing the lyrics will be lost

Part of me is aware
You already packed and moved away
Without saying goodbye
And the song you once sang
Likely died

Oh dear child
You never danced in the sun
You would dance with it
You could tell the sky was trying not to turn dark
As the ridgid mountains pushed the night away
In an attempt to spare you from the darkness
But you would dance with the moon too
A spotlight
To guide you along
A stage made up of mysteriously perfect grass
You talked as if the past didn't phase you

You never experienced
Abandoning the light
Until the mountains folded
Forcing the moonlight out early
Hoping to let you rest

Little me does not exist anymore
The world became too much for her
So here I am in her place
For I am her representation
Though I fear I disappointed

Snapped

When we were younger
We would beg and scream to stay up
Playing in the light of the moon
Using it as a way to defend our childhood
Now we're tossing and turning
Like how butter is made
As days go on
My eyes feel like they are carrying pounds
Of the sweet sensation of sugar
Though this time it's sour
And the cream that the butter was made from
Has spoiled

So what night
Was our guard let down
Our weapons put away

What night
Were we attacked
Defeated

What night
Were we no longer
Allowed to play

Your first breath
Replicated calm valleys of lilacs
But you were never expecting a battle
That dictated your decisions
To prevent you from admiring the beauty
That your childhood held

You ran for cover in a broken structure
That sat in the middle of the field
Yet you were still struck
As you were never protected
Just teased to reside in the comfort of the thought

Do not rush age
As it will strike you
Within arms of a child
Who can no longer hold you

I have gone to war
Protecting my childhood

Yet as age bashed against my ribs
I was enclosed in the trench of growth
Unable to escape the chaos

A bloody massacre
Succumbing me to the nature of age

A defeat
Where recovery was not an option

Do not undermine the torment of exclusion
Held in unwelcoming air
As its rejection
Smells of thick gasoline
Often the hardest to breathe in
Like the panicked roar of an engine
Underneath the hood of a car
Our cries are internal
Our decay hidden
Although we are still suffering
Despite if you can see it
Or not

Anna O'Reilly

Am I unlovable
Or is my existence a disease
Others run from
I never meant to cause a pandemic

Constantly locked
Out of the gates of relationships
Aware of my existence
Yet constantly ignored
If not avoided

I am pushed to the outside
Condemned to a glass vial
Absent of their view
Although never hidden from their judgment
As words are still spoken
Avast my presence

At what point do I wonder
Can I make a vaccine for myself

I have downed each vile of the poison I used to fear

Self-sabotage was never bitter
It hid the myth of innocence
Brought to light the fear of a storm
Developing inside a tranquil dream

For a nightmare was never expected
When I was told I could be whatever I wanted

One second
I'm driving through reality
On clear streets
With music turned high
Windows down
My hair to the wind
Full freedom in my path
As the stress of tomorrow is blown away
Roads of my future have become clear

Until 20 seconds later

When the sirens start to blare
I can barely breathe
With the glass of change stabbed within my neck
On my knees
Bleeding out of spite
As my future has been masked
In a hazed fog of anxiety
For even the thought of stability
Is uncertain

Oh Mother Nature
I fear I took your job
As my reality changes
Like snow in December

Clear until time turns
Beauty into slush

I have caused storms during sunny days
As my anxiety has only produced clouds
Blocking the light from reaching me

I'm constantly stuck in mud season
Unable to escape my worries for the future

Mother Nature please take over
I'm ready to be freed
From the responsibilities
I never meant to steal

How can a season
Turn your coffee cold
Turn your content
Into a brisk air
That never fails to leave

How can a season
Bring memories of laughter
Along with the taste
Of a burn on your tongue
A flavor so strong
Even sugar can't fix

How can a season
Bring leaves that cannot speak
But also tell me all of their disguises
Waiting for me to
Fall

How can a season
Announce the color of rain
I was told I would dance through
Depicting my childhood passions
But also extract it
As it no longer
Falls
With color

A Box Of Broken Crayons

I live in a jungle
One contained to four walls
Holding vines you can't swing on
A floor littered
With clothes and trash from last month

Tacks cover the walls
A parasite
Leaving holes in the wood
Though no trees could grow here

All-natural light has been blocked by creativity
Replaced with neon signs
And LEDs that always stay the same color
The sky does not have a sun
But a daughter that it watches over

The plants are all fake except for the cactus
Even that is dying
Despite the abundance of cups
We are in a drought
No energy to scream
Just to rot
This jungle is my home inside a house

If I am locked inside myself
Trust me when I say
Let me be

I will do with the pain
Turn it to static
Replace the hurt
With peace
And change the channel

I own a light
Woven of the wax
Once defined by my parents
Who spoke with the perfection of labor
Concealing ambition inside me
Planted
Under the snow-stung bridge of lost connection
Driving me further into my own accomplishments
Grown
Amidst the stranded glacier-laced gardens of solitude
Guiding me down a restless path of determination
Blown out
Washed by everlasting winter
As radiance was outlawed
In the grasp of perpetual frost
Relit
Despite the frozen eternity

A dream cannot completely elapse
With an open heart
Whose lock can never be iced over

The fingers once creating art
Have become the project

Seared with graphite burns
Written with the brush of anxiety
For the hard work is shown through my wounds
As blood became my paint

I have drawn a thousand stairs
Stood on each one
To admire the rest from a different perspective

Yet I still fear
Success does not want these ruined hands
For they are so damaged by labor
That I have been committed to the failures of my past

My system of nostalgia
Held in the smallest stars
Hidden in constellations
Inside my body of cells
That entangled itself into my spinal cord

While my comfort was a tumor
Once engulfed in the same journey
Until it was extracted
By the scalpel of words that strangers held
Paralysing me in a world of distrust

You will learn
That there is no pain
Harsher than being replaced
By the people who told you they would never leave

Watching the chain of your heart snap
Despite being told
It was unbreakable

The worst part is
If you acknowledge it
You automatically have caused destruction
As you will always be the villain
To those who have hurt you

They say to drop the toxic people from your life

But you cannot tell poison from water
Until you're already dying
          – Who knew poison tasted so organic

The sweet little girl
Who feared fitting in
Now drinks the water of shadows
Praying not to be
Seen
Heared
Or acknowledged

The child inside her
Stopped handcrafting each thought
Unable to keep up with demands
Forced to open a factory
Paid for
With the spark
She stole from her younger self

The mirror is a psychopath
Manipulating us into
The addiction of our reflection

Providing our younger versions
The satisfaction of beauty
Causing us to constantly ask for its approval

Its response has since turned cold
Holding hands of reflection
To point out all our flaws
Despite once providing an illusion of beauty

Yet running away is no longer an option
It follows
Stalking us through the beauty of running streams
Dressing rooms
And store windows

Though maybe it's not the mirror
We struggle to accept
As the mirror is not only a vision of reflection
But an imitation of the mind that changes with it

Anna O'Reilly

I dare you to look into your eyes
Do you see the shades
Of all your tears
A pallet that only grows deeper
The longer you stare

You are no longer a child
Who screeches
Lets water flow
All because of a stubbed toe

As each shade of life
Is one that opens the dam
To the river in your eyes

A stream that flows backwards
As you have blocked off the waterfall
Causing a drought on your cheeks

I cannot see your reflection
Only your insecurities
~ My Mirror

If I hand you crayons
To touch up
Color in my wings
You look at me
Like I am out of place

A realization floods my core
I have only seen my reflection
Inside a crystal
Appearing a rainbow to myself
Admiring natural beauty

Although
You only know me as a moth
Observing my peers as butterflies

Do not open the window
Expecting me to fly

My wings have been sprained
Held down by rocks of fear
Mixed with sticks of the idea
That by setting flight
I will become the sight of failure

I reside in a box of crayons
Not yet tampered
Or disturbed
Bonded to the distinct colors of childhood
Scents that never fail to set me free

I smell of chalk
Etched into a late summer's evening
That leaves marks of blended color on my hands

I smell of my first soccer goal
On an early Saturday morning
Leaving victory in my skin
Along with the stains of adrenaline on my knees

I smell of colors I was not born with
But learned to mix myself

A Box Of Broken Crayons

Inside my box of crayons
I hold memories in each color
That put the charade of life into an explosion

Each year I would be given a new box
Of what looked like perfection
But drew the opposite color

Anna O'Reilly

My home is not one color
It's the color of my tears
And smiles combined

It's not only yellow
But also gray

It's the color of a bee sting
With the flavor of late-night drives

It's more than the colors in a rainbow
It's everything in between
If it was one color
My home would not be me

A Box Of Broken Crayons

I dislike the smell of reality
It lacks tones of creativity
And replaces them with a heart
That contradicts my brain

I will stick to the perfume of my imagination
Even though it's a scent others call delusion
It's an improvement
From the air built of age

I do not understand a world
Absent of anxiety

How can someone walk down
A path I must run
Only to beat my fears

How can someone observe a sunset
In colors of safety
While I am only aware
Of the blood inside my thoughts

How can someone sleep
While I am tired of being held inside
A coffin of panic
Screaming that I am still alive

How can someone refuse to see
That anxiety
Is a knife
My child was stabbed with
And told not to bleed

Dear Compassion
I have always loved you
But you make it hard for me to heal

You caused a fire
Inside my own veins
Creating a burning sense
Of blame
In others harm towards me

Without any information
On how to kill the flames

Do not donate your heart like a kidney
Do not provide only because someone asks
You are not a charity case
Whose purpose is to drain your veins
For strangers
As they have never been an IV

For the blood
That has been displaced from your heart
Is not your fault
For you have been stabbed with insecurity
Placed by others
And I do not have the eyes to watch you bleed out

I love you
Words spoken enough times to flood the sea
Yet my heart is still a dessert
As my mind carries tides of doubt
Filled with fear of sharks in the water

Despite this
Don't be surprised when it starts to rain
I will collect each drop of water
Ensuring that there is enough
To give you a feeling of love
That will soon crash into your heart

How can you lose the memory of true love
For age is a needle that unstitches every thread
To leave bloody holes inside your fingertips
And unknit weaves

This needle harmed more than a piece of fabric
It has taken away the connections made
Stripped me of each piece of love I have felt
For I am sewing away all feeling
To share with those whose string was cut
Yet I am missing one strand

I am currently trying to find the thread
Of true love inside myself

Hello
This is the "little kid" you once were
I walked through each section to reach you
With a question in mind
Do you hate me
Or did you forget you're still my role model
I bought a house inside of your heart
With a contract signing away all ability of freedom
As I did not think you were capable
Of causing someone so much pain
Yet I ended up as a victim of your crimes

As each insult you engineered upon yourself
Each form of self-doubt
Were the blades inside my heart
Searching for my arteries
Sacrificing the knives from your own kitchen

You were once the person I was excited to meet
And well I could never hate you
I do wish I had the chance to move

Dear Age
Do you have a second to listen

You used to tell me I could rule the sea
Yet you have only turned me into
A ship of spilling water
Taken inside the mercy of the waves
Causing me to be ripped from my throne
Dragged towards a whirlpool of fear

As a child I was never scared
Believing that the tide would shift
Eventually throwing me on land
Before I was sucked down

Though I do not see any beaches
Only spirals of water
Entering through my mouth
Causing me to plead for my childhood

Though even if you take me
You must know
I am still a child
Just one that has been dethroned

You stand
A statue
Refusing to age
Hidden in the belief
That your life is planned inside your child's eyes
As you convinced yourself
Age was an experience that would never affect you
Only a thought
That held you
Suffocating under soil
Despite the knowledge that
Like a plant
You were not ready to be picked
As you were still sprouting
Never believing you would soon blossom

I am the disciple of my parents
For I will someday live in a land I am yet to know
With strangers who currently walk the streets
Without my name in mind
A time I am scared to confront

Here I am content
I have orange trees that fill the air with a citrus scent
Here I have love
Out there I fear hatred

Let me find the embrace of life
On the terms that fit me best
So in a world of constant worrying
I will cheer at each opportunity that comes my way

But in 10 years
My life will be blue
Well these years
Drift to gray

Only the clouds will know why
The adrenaline of childhood
Lost the race of time

A Box Of Broken Crayons

From your first breath
You hung to your parents' legs for answers
Wanting to know every detail in the book about you
One you did not write
Holding a narrative you were unaware of
It was a picture book that was read too quickly
With illustrations you created

As the realisation hit
You must write the sequel

Your parents' next version would be filled with
Uncertainty
Causing a book of fiction

Did you notice
How quickly they became the ones with questions
As you hold the answers to your
Past
Present
And soon your future

You were always an author
Just one that had not written the story down

Anna O'Reilly

I am lost inside a story with no plot
Chaos ensues throughout each page
For the rest of the book seems
Long
Ripped
Unfinished
Though each word is handcrafted
In a story only I can write
For I will not break my narrative like a crayon
As I can't stand another cliffhanger

We cannot look at our surroundings
Through the simple lens
Of good and evil

We are all villains
In someone's story
Despite being a victim in our own
And a hero in someone else's

An idea we must accept
Before we get confused
And lost
In the world of our own
Character development

To Age
I know you are a thief
Yet I have forgotten all that you have taken from me
Ironic
As you stole my memory

If you don't mind
Would you remind me of the last time I rode my bike
Or the last time I played with my Barbies
How about the last time
I cried being sent to my room
Maybe you remember my last soccer game
What about the last time mom picked out my clothes
Cause I can't seem to remember

So stop swatting my hand away
When I try to grasp onto the time I have young
As I am trying to brand it all into my bones
Petrified that you will lead me blind
Into my last opportunity

Strangers lurk the walls
As the time ahead of us turns to reality
Crumpling inside my lungs

For two years from now
I will never breathe the same air
As the strangers
I once told my life story to

I wish I could explain to time
The pain it causes me
As I'm convinced
Survival without them
Is near impossible

Anna O'Reilly

I attached to myself at a young age
Thinking I could never possibly leave
　　　　- Perhaps I was wrong

A Box Of Broken Crayons

I am loved
I am admired
I am nurtured

Not by my future
But the child of my past
She picks up the glass littered where I step
Where my future is the one who scattered the shards

Anna O'Reilly

Worn Down

I am lost
On the road I grew up on
I can no longer see my childhood
Formed in the backyard
The boiling slide
Boken jungle gym
Taken without a trace
If I squint I can see little me
Running around as if nothing has changed
She's a spirit
Who does not imagine leaving

Years to her
A bystander
Only watching
Refusing to intervene

I'd like to hope
That time has empathy
For pieces of us that we never get to see

Though I still struggle to welcome it
As things that lack emotion
Feel impossible to forgive

I have tread a land unknown to me
Although my parents have already seen these trees

I am a land of Deja Vu for the plants
That watch for someone new
The water has already been drunk
I do not feel welcome

It was known there was no way back
For it was a one-way path
That seemed to be walked through twice

Call the name of the daisies
Not the roses
For their thorns have just been sharpened
By blades of grass
Their faces show evil
Masked with a sugar-coating

They see my empathy
But I don't hear them call out
I only feel their grasp leading me towards hell
Though I must resist their petals
Dyed by the color of their last victim's flesh

Something that beautiful
Can't be so pure
Especially if you're unaware
Of the thorns that lie underneath

I learned my lesson last time
To not go picking roses
For the blood is not worth the picture

To the next version of me
I spoke to your origin the other day
They spoke highly of you
As they turned you into a god
Exclaiming you had survived meteors
Climbed volcanos
Became the spitting image of their imagination

Unfortunately
They do not know you
 If they did
They would know
You hold bones of steel
And a heart mixed to perfection
You grew up in this world
And that is more impressive
Than any meteors you survived
Or volcanos you climbed
Your old self
Would bow in your presence
As meeting you
Is an honor

I took flight along the blue cloud-freckled sky
Unaware of my fear for the future
My bow
Shot blind
With micro-cracks along the point

I knew the outcome would slice me open
Crack me in half even
I was foolish
Never trusting the world
To bring me this far

Perhaps I will never get there
Maybe the wind threw me off-track
Either way
I question how I made it off the ground
A dream I never thought would leave my bow

Now I can see the area where I will land
As my thoughts of downfall
Marked the land where my weapon will crash

Follow your needs to a tea
Avoid the details that feel like coffee
I have found they lead to a more bitter path
~ The diner two blocks away

The strings are all loose
The instrument is tired
It's no longer gold
Quickly turning to brass
With maroon tints of rust

Weird to think that years ago
I thought the sound would last
But it has been overused
Teased by the dreams
That I think I knew would never come true

This priceless creation
Now can't even be sold for a dime
Yet I would pay thousands
Just to keep it as mine

If my tongue does not allow
Holding a voice

If my lips do not tear
Open

If my lungs do not breathe
Lasting air

If my hands do not type
Down ideas

If my heart does not sing
Orbiting societies expectations

Then they say
No one can glare

I have never heard a more false statement
Others' glares are because we are human
Silencing yourself
Is not going to make you alien

Life will create fear
If you use your time
To look through
Thin lines
Seeing a blade
Thirsty for a river of red
For death has never been far behind

That's why we held excitement that made us blind
You never thought about the end
When you were riding bikes along the road
Or swimming in bellowing creeks
Never questioned it when
You were scream-singing your favorite songs
Windows down as you drove through rocky roads
With your hair caught in the night's wind
So why care when you're alone

I talked to death the other day
Part of its intentions are sinister
To captivate all your thoughts
So instead look towards the life you have left
And prove to death that you have a life worth living

What if one day we awake
With no recollection of who we are

What language did we speak
Was it the language of love
That coursed through our hearts
Deep into our souls
Did we know the language of anger
The fury that filled us with hatred
Did we speak the tears of our anxiety
The hesitation that stopped us from colliding
Did we ever learn the grief of loss
The pain that had us collapsing in a field
Trying to hold on
What if we forgot...

Fades

To

Gray

My first breath came with tears of the unknown
My last will end in the knowledge of my successes
Ensure that on my face lies a smile
Before I am covered in the blood of my town

For I have caused change in this world
Even if it was once my biggest fear

Death must be like the fresh air earth never held
Something no one is allergic to

We must remember
Death cannot cause itself
It's the aftermath of suffrage
That we know carries uncertainty

We fear more about where our souls go
Than the idea of leaving the world

Yet why fear something
We have no control over
As it is inevitable
And our anxiety
Will not make it go away

But even after our acceptance
It still leaves us with lungs of existential dread
As the knowledge that it was unstoppable
Was never the only piece
That made it scary

I am unaware of my own beliefs
That come to life after
I step on my last leaf
Or give my last hug
As I arrive at a dead end
Yet I hope there is still a chance
To remain in this world
In whatever form is needed
But I don't hate the idea of it being something new
So why do I stress when I don't care the outcome

Maybe it's the pain
The thought that it might last forever
Maybe it's the idea of hell
Not knowing the true rubric on which it's graded
Maybe it's an idea I have not thought of yet
One worse than the human mind can craft
Maybe it's the idea that after death I will lose
Everyone I have crafted relationships with
Including myself

But in the end
Losing people is the only piece of structure
In information that does not stand still

Do you understand the feeling of disruption

When the world doesn't stop
But we are stuck

When the pain of death becomes an afterthought
Even if there is no after

When you turn away from the future
But it comes anyway

Do you understand that the world
Will not listen
Despite the millions of screams
Pleading for its mercy
Earth was not given ears to hear
Or a mouth to respond
Only a body
To keep us alive
Well some choose to use it for war

Let death not separate our minds
You may tread softly on without me
Though you will never be alone

Goodbye is not a word beyond the grave
It's a saying of displeasure
That shows the mistreatment of history
As the world will carry on

Although my memory may be heavy
Please don't put me down

We will one day hear the business of the kettle break
For the last time
As the chime is no longer a greeting
It's a whisper of farewell
That writes the last chapter
In a book I never understood

Let death not be the leader in every thought
Full prevention is not an option
We shall let it pass
Like a mistake that in the end
Will already be all that we remember
Let's not make it the only memory held by others

Don't watch the ink empty
Examine the words you're writing instead

Rather than fearing death
Why not look to the sky

Think of its beauty
As an escape
From a world
That never wiped our tears

Death is something even the weak can do
Although only the strong are able to find
Romance inside it

If you've ever attempted to stop a wave
Finding temporary disruption
Was your best attempt
You already understand death

Comprehending that
Tidal waves
Are not forecast to stop
Being hit is inevitable
Despite your attempted delays

Soon the news of your death
Will be washed over

As people have become too comfortable with the
"Cycle of life"
To the point where
Others have been drowned
By those who became the wave

She is at her strongest
When death dresses in her clothes
Speaking her language
With words she doesn't know
Yet discussed through the comfort of her demise

Her blood flows thinner with every passing day
Before she found the reaper
And let him lead the way

A Box Of Broken Crayons

I am a tourist of my mind
Though one that never leaves

I will sit
Watch as the colors shift
With abandoned buildings fading gray
Attractions have become places I run from

I have stayed in this ghost town
While others wander off
I have no place to go

I have never seen the exit
Others speak so highly of
For my grave has already been crafted
In the same soil
I walk on each morning
As I am aware I will lie in this town

After my passing
Will the exit make itself known
Or only take away the oxygen
That made this place bearable

Ready to be buried in my favorite season
Though they cannot find my bones
Lost for centuries
As they hold the pain and beauty
In every aspect of my life

They have searched every morgue
Dug at every inch of soil in this land

I guess I was never meant to be buried whole
As the majority of me
Is found in the things I love

A Box Of Broken Crayons

The sand castle I once built
Now a cracked hourglass
With sand sifting through my fingertips
Shards of glass chipping the spirit of my child
Until she bleeds of silence

For this beach that used to burn her toes
As she danced among the dunes
Holds the same sand that covers her

Life may only be a snippet
Of what you were meant to achieve
But learning to live in it
Is the hardest part

We have no instructions to guide our path
For we are stragglers on a trail
That ends in a dead-end

Our hands will eventually
Become crossed inside a box
The only time we begin to understand a stage of life
The first time we see a piece of clarity
Crafted without a pen
But rather with a soul of sugar and lemon

Though despite this
Even after we have lived through each chapter
We're still left on a cliffhanger
Not knowing what comes next